YOUR KNOWLEDGE HAS VALUE

Bibliographic information published by the German National Library:

The German National Library lists this publication in the National Bibliography; detailed bibliographic data are available on the Internet at http://dnb.dnb.de .

Imprint:

Copyright © 2015 GRIN Verlag, Open Publishing GmbH
Print and binding: Books on Demand GmbH, Norderstedt Germany
ISBN: 978-3-668-03713-7

This book at GRIN:

http://www.grin.com/en/e-book/303631/reading-log-of-the-fault-in-our-stars-by-john-green

Leopold Pfeiffer

Reading Log of "The Fault in Our Stars" by John Green

GRIN Publishing

GRIN - Your knowledge has value

Since its foundation in 1998, GRIN has specialized in publishing academic texts by students, college teachers and other academics as e-book and printed book. The website www.grin.com is an ideal platform for presenting term papers, final papers, scientific essays, dissertations and specialist books.

Visit us on the internet:

http://www.grin.com/

http://www.facebook.com/grincom

http://www.twitter.com/grin_com

Reading Log by
Leopold Pfeiffer

Table of contents

The background of the book's front cover is light blue. There are two big clouds, a white one and a black one, which are the things you recognize first. The title, "The Fault in Our Stars", is written in the black cloud and the name of the author, John Green, is written in the white cloud. The font resembles the fog in the clouds, which makes it very suitable for the rest of the cover. Altogether, the front cover looks like a sky with some clouds. Above the two clouds is a yellow dot and it says that the book is a No. 1 New York Times bestseller. This is kind of an advertisement because the publisher of the book wants you to think that the book must be good as it is a bestseller. At the bottom there is a quote from a famous German-Australian author, Markus Zusak. He tells us about the feelings he had while reading the book and that he wanted to read more books by John Green.

On the back cover, there is one quote from the famous newspaper "Time", which tells us how good the book is. The next paragraph is kind of an advertisement as well. Again, the designer of the book cover wants us to think it is an incredible good book. The last paragraph summarizes the plot very roughly. We can guess that Hazel and Augustus fall in love, although it is not written in the text.

As I have already seen the movie and read the book as well, I know what the plot is about and I know that I like it. When I went to the cinema to watch the movie, I was a bit sceptical because I normally do not like dramatic and sentimental films but afterwards I was very impressed how good it is and it was actually the first movie I have ever nearly started to cry. A few months later I decided to buy the book because one of my friends told me that it is pretty good. Again, I was very sceptical because I did not want to read the book in case I do not like it as much as I liked the movie. I was not sure, whether the author could describe the story as good as it is described in the movie and I thought that I would not like the book at all if it was not as great as the film. Another thing I was not really sure about was that I do not read a lot of fictional books. I mean I do read a lot but mostly no made up stories. Obviously there was a lot of doubt whether to read it or not but finally I ended up reading it – and I did not regret it.

24/05/15	• Chapter 1 - 2
25/05/15	• Chapter 3 - 12
26/05/15	• Chapter 13 - 14
29/05/15	• Chapter 15 - 21
30/05/15	• Chapter 22 - 25

The book starts with a quote from the book that is mentioned in "The Fault in Our Stars", *An Imperial Affliction*. The quote is about a man looking at the sea. He sees the waves and the water as a metaphor for time.

Chapter One (24/05/15)
The main character, Hazel Graze Lancaster, a girl suffering from terminal cancer, lives with her parents. Her mom makes her attend a support group for children and teenagers who are diagnosed with cancer as well. She meets Augustus Water there, who has joined the group because of his friend Isaac, who attends the group as well. Augustus and Hazel get to meet each other and he invites her to his house to watch a movie with an actress, who looks like Hazel Graze according to Augustus.

Chapter Two (24/05/15)
Augustus drives with Hazel to his house. On the way, Hazel Graze explains her cancer story to Augustus. When they arrive at the house, Gus's parents are cooking. They welcome Hazel and the two teenagers go downstairs into the basement, aka Gus's room, to talk. Hazel makes Gus read her favourite book, *An Imperial Affliction* and she promises to read one of Gus's books. After that they watch *V for Vendetta*, a pretty famous movie. At the end of the chapter they say goodbye and say that they would catch up soon.

Chapter Three (25/05/15)
The next morning, Hazel's mom wakes her up because it is her thirty-third half-birthday, which means she turns 16 and a half years old. To celebrate the day, Hazel Graze meets up with her old school friend Kaitlyn. They hang out in a shopping centre and talk about anything and afterwards they go shopping. After Kaitlyn leaves, Hazel buys the second book of the book series Gus fancies.

Chapter Four (25/05/15)
Hazel starts reading *An Imperial Affliction* again and we get to know what the book is about. It is about Anna, who has cancer and the book ends in the middle of a sentence because Anna probably dies. Because Hazel Graze wants to know what happens after the ending of the book she wants to track down the author. After a while Hazel calls Augustus and because she realizes that Isaac is with him and apparently very depressed and sad, she comes over to help. When she arrives, Gus tells her that Isaac and his girlfriend broke up. As a therapy Augustus offers Isaac to destroy all of his basketball trophies.

Chapter Five (25/05/15)
After a while Gus calls Hazel and tells her what he thinks about *An Imperial Affliction*. He also loves the book and they talk about it for quite a while. Somehow Augustus contacted Van Houten, the author, and he surprises Hazel with an email he got from Van Houten's assistant. At the end of the phone call they discover "Okay" as kind of a promise to each other, like Monica and Isaac used to say "always". Hazel writes an email to Van Houten and asks him to give her some information about what happens after the end of her favourite book. In this chapter Isaac has his operation as well and gets blind because of that. The next morning Hazel Graze gets an answer from Van Houten, who tells her that he could impossibly write about the ending of the book but he offers her to talk about it if

she ever finds herself in Amsterdam, where he lives. At the end of the chapter Gus offers her his "Genie Wish", a wish that all children with cancer get from an organisation and because Hazel has already used her wish for a trip to Disney World, Augustus wants to take her on a Trip to Amsterdam.

Chapter Six (25/05/15)
Home again, Hazel tells her parents about Gus's generous offer to take her to Amsterdam. They are both not sure whether that is a good idea because of her disease. She is very sad and also confused about her feelings for Augustus. After she checked the Facebook page of Gus's ex-girlfriend, who died of cancer, she decides not to risk hurting him, too. At dinner she bursts and tells her parents that she is like a grenade that is about to explode and kill everything around it. Later this evening, her parents come to her room and talk about it and say that they do not see her as a grenade, but love her without any exceptions. Hazel finally falls asleep but the next morning she wakes up and has a massive headache.

Chapter Seven (25/05/15)
Hazel Graze's parents take her to the hospital right away and she faints. Later, she wakes up in the ICU alone. She learns that the headache was not caused by a brain tumour, but by fluid in her lungs. She has to spend six more days in the hospital until she is finally allowed to go home. Augustus, who has been waiting the whole time in the hospital, can talk to her and he tels her that the trip to the Netherlands is not possible until she gets better. Hazel does not accept that and asks her mom right away if she could go to Amsterdam.

Chapter Eight (25/05/15)
Hazel attends a Cancer Group Meeting with all her doctors and they discuss her current situation. At the end of the meeting, Hazel asks whether she can go to Amsterdam and two of the three doctors say that it is okay but one is against it because he doesn't want to risk anything. Hazel is incredibly sad that she can't go and she calls Augustus. They meet up and Augustus tries to comfort her. The next morning Hazel receives an email from Van Houten's assistant, who tells her that everything is set up for her trip next week. Hazel tells her mom that they have to tell Van Houten that they won't come but her mom tells her that the trip is actually on and the doctors agreed to let her go.

Chapter Nine (25/05/15)
One day before the trip to the Netherlands, Hazel Graze Lancaster decides to go to the support group one more time. She meets Isaac there and a girl, who tells her that Hazel inspires her. Hazel's answer is not very friendly: She tells the girl that she would like to have her remission. But, being Hazel, she feels guilty about it right after she said it. After support group, Hazel and Isaac go to Isaac's house where they play a video game for blind people. Hazel tells Isaac about her doubts that she does not want to risk hurting Augustus.

Chapter Ten (25/05/15)
The day of the trip to Amsterdam has finally arrived. Hazel and her mom leave after breakfast and the farewell with her dad is pretty sad. He breaks out into tears because he is probably afraid that it is the last time he can see his daughter. They arrive at Gus's house and they hear loud voices inside. Obviously Augustus is fighting with his mother. After a while he leaves the house and seems like nothing has happened. For Augustus it is the first flight in an airplane so he is very nervous. On the plane the two teenagers talk about a lot of different things. Hazel recites a poem and suddenly Augustus tells her that he is in love with her. She doesn't answer to that.

Chapter Eleven (25/05/15)

The group arrives in Amsterdam and Hazel takes a nap because she is very tired from the flight. She wakes up after a while and her mother tells her that she has reserved a table for her daughter and Augustus in a very fancy restaurant. In the restaurant they enjoy the incredible good food and they are really surprised when they figure out that Van Houten pays for the dinner. After dinner they go for a walk along the canal and finally they sit down on a bench. When Hazel leans against Augustus he howls with pain. We don't get to know why. Augustus tells Hazel everything about his relationship with Caroline. He tells her that she was actually very mean to him but he thinks that the brain tumour has changed her. Hazel tells her that she is afraid of hurting him. Gus's answer is that "would be a privilege to have his heart broken by her."

Chapter Twelve (25/05/15)

Hazel and Augustus will meet Van Houten and ask him the questions they have been thinking of for so long. In the morning, Hazel decides to dress like Anna from *An Imperial Affliction*. Gus and Hazel go to Van Houten's apartment and knock at the door very excitedly. An old man opens the door but shuts it again a moment later. The two young people hear someone shouting inside. The voice wants them to leave. A moment later, the door opens again and they enter the house. Augustus and Hazel try to start a normal conversation with Van Houten but he only cares about his drink. Apparently he is very drunk. He only answers on the question what happened to the hamster but he doesn't tell them any other information. He ends up insulting Hazel Graze and Augustus. Lidewij, Van Houten's assistant, tells him to shut up and resigns her job because he doesn't stop. Gus finally leads Hazel outside the house where she breaks out into tears. He tries to comfort her and promises to write an epilogue to the book for her. As an apology Lidewij offers them to show them the Anne Frank House. Hazel is still angry and very sad. Inside the house she tries to prove to herself that she can do things without any help and climbs all the stairs. Although she nearly faints a couple of times, they finally reach the top level of the building. Augustus and Hazel Graze start flirting and eventually they kiss each other. After they visited the house the two teenagers go back to the hotel, where they have sex. The next morning, Hazel draws a diagram that shows Gus's loss of virginity:

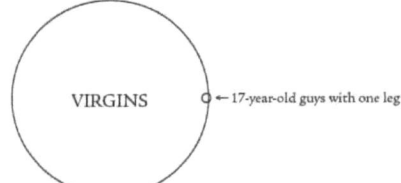

Abbildung 1: http://data.whicdn.com/images/49520835/tumblr_mgkbyx72ro1s1aktqo1_500_large.jpg

Chapter Thirteen (26/05/15)

The next day Hazel and Augustus tell Hazel's mom a funnier story of what happened at Van Houten's house – but they leave out the kiss and the sex. Hazel and Gus go for a walk and sit down. Augustus tells Hazel Graze that he had another PET scan before they left...and his cancer has returned. They are both incredibly devastated and they both cry. The cancer was also the reason for the fight Gus had with his mom when Hazel arrived at his house. She didn't want him to go because in Amsterdam he couldn't get his Chemo treatment. Hazel tells him that now he has to fight the cancer. In the end they make out.

Chapter Fourteen (26/05/15)

On the flight back, Gus feels the pain of the cancer in his chest. He takes pills and falls asleep. Back in the states, Hazel's dad welcomes them. At home, Hazel has a very deep talk with her dad, who read *An Imperial Affliction*, while she was away. They talk about the universe and how it wants to be noticed. The next day, Hazel and Isaac hang up at Gus's house. Isaac is still messed up because Monica dumped him, so Augustus thinks they have to take revenge. They drive to her house and Isaac, still being blind, tries to throw eggs at her car. After some failures he finally succeeds and they have a lot of fun. While the boys are vancalizing, Hazel takes a picture of them and we find out that it is the last picture she will ever take of Augustus.

Chapter Fifteen *(29/05/15)*
At dinner with their parents, Gus and Hazel still talk about the fancy food they had in the restaurant in Amsterdam. But the good mood gets destroyed when Augustus has to go to the emergency room a week later. Hazel Graze wants to visit him but Gus's mom tells her that although she loves Hazel she wants this to be a family moment. Hazel understands it and waits for Gus in the waiting room. After Augustus is allowed to leave the hospital again, he and his girlfriend go to the "Funky Bones Park" where they have been before.

Chapter Sixteen *(29/05/15)*
Hazel develops a habit of visiting Augustus every day to hang out with him, talk to him, play video games with him and things like that. Augustus tells her that he still thinks of writing an epilogue to *An Imperial Affliction* but he is too tired and sick to do so.

Chapter Seventeen *(29/05/15)*
Hazel and Gus are back from the Netherlands for one month now. Hazel visits Gus in the morning and when she enters is bedroom she recognizes that he's wet himself at night. Augustus finds out that Hazel saw it and gets incredibly embarrassed. He tells her that he has always strived for an extraordinary life, which is worth remembering and also a heroic obituary. Hazel tells him that she wants him to write an obituary for her.

Chapter Eighteen *(29/05/15)*
At 2 a.m., Hazel wakes up because her phone is ringing. It's Gus and Hazel s terrified that he has died and his mom wants to tell her. She answers the phone but instead of Gus's mom, Gus himself is talking. He tells her that he s at the gas station and something with his G-tube is wrong. He tells her not to call the police or anyone else. Hazel doesn't hesitate, gets in the car and rushes to the gas station. She realizes that Augustus's G-tube is extremely infected. She pulls out her phone but Gus tells her to stop. She calls the police though. Augustus completely brakes into tears; he tells her that he hates his life, himself and he just wants to die. Hazel holds him and recites a poem until he faints.

Chapter Nineteen *(29/05/15)*
After Gus gets home from hospital, it is really hard for him to leave the bed. Hazel is at his house nearly every day and tries to comfort him. She talks a lot with his parents as well. On day Gus wants to go outside with Hazel. He tells her there, that he is unbelievably grateful for her.

Chapter Twenty *(29/05/15)*
Gus calls Hazel and tells her that he'd like her to come over to the place where they had the support group meetings. When she wants to leave she starts a fight with her parents because they feel like they never see her because she is at Gus's. It turns into a really rough fight but when Hazel tells her parents that Augustus is about to die, they don't say anything else. She leaves the house and goes to the church where she meets Gus and Isaac. Gus explains that he wants to witness his own funeral. Isaac starts with his eulogy It is mostly about Gus being arrogant but in a very ironic but still very sad

way. In the end, Isaac starts to cry. Now it's Hazel Graze's turn. She talks about some infinities being larger than other infinities and about the infinity she had with Augustus. She starts to cry as well.

Chapter Twenty-one (29/05/15)
One night, Hazel Graze gets a phone call. It is Gus's mom. He died.
Of course, Hazel Graze is devastated and unbelievably sad. Her parents really don't know how to help her. She reads through all the Facebook post and Augustus's Facebook page. Everyone is writing about how they already miss him, even though – in Hazel's opinion – they never cared about him before. She writes a post as well, to which no one responds. In the end of the chapter she watches TV with her parents.

Chapter Twenty-two (30/05/15)
It's the day of Augustus's funeral and Hazel is there. She watches all the people saying goodbye to Gus in the coffin. She goes to the coffin as well and kisses him on the cheek. Before she goes back to the others she puts a pack of cigarettes into the coffin. After that it's the service. Hazel sits there and suddenly realizes that Van Houten sits behind her. She listens to Isaac, giving his eulogy and then gives hers as well. It's not the same eulogy she gave when she, Gus and Isaac were in the church. She changes it completely and talks about the encouragements in Gus's house. After the service, she thinks of not going to the funeral but decides to go because she knows it is the right thing to do. After the burial, Van Houten wants to get in Hazel's parents' car. He talks about really weird stuff like cells being born from other cells. It's enough for Hazel. She tells him to leave the car because he is an alcoholic and a psychopath. The family gets home and Hazel goes into the bathroom and locks the door. Her dad comes in and tells her, that even though it was a short period of time, it was a privilege to love Augustus and that he feels the same about her.

Chapter Twenty-three (30/05/15)
A few days later, Hazel goes to Isaac's house. They play his video game for blind people and they talk about how much they miss Augustus. Isaac asks Hazel whether she got the thing Gus wrote for her. She doesn't know what he is talking about. She decides to go to Augustus's house to look for it. When she gets in the car she realizes that Peter Van Houten sits in the back seat. She tells him to get out of the car but he ignores her. He tells her that she reminds him of Anna, the girl who suffers from cancer in the book. He apologizes for ruining the trip to Amsterdam and he starts crying about Augustus. That's when Hazel realizes that he must have had someone in his family who died of cancer. He admits that it was his daughter who died. Hazel recommends that he should go home, stop drinking and write another book. He tells her that she is right but while he's saying that he sips at his bottle of booze. After Van Houten left the car, Hazel gets to Gus's house and she asks his parents whether she could go into his room. She can't find what she was looking for, so she lays into his bed to smell his scent.

Chapter Twenty-four (30/05/15)
Augustus's dad calls Hazel and tells her that he found a notebook but that a few pages are missing. Hazel thinks that he might have hid them in the support group church. She can't find them and goes home. At home she has a fight with her mom about food. Her mom wants her do eat dinner but Hazel claims that she is not hungry. She tells her mom that it doesn't matter whether she eats or not because she is dying anyway. She also tells her that she can't do anything about her mom not being a mother anymore after her death. She tells her that she is afraid that after her death, her parents

won't know how to go on. Her mom finally admits that she is taking classes to get a master's degree in social work. She didn't tell her because she was afraid that Hazel is angry because her parents think about a life without her. But Hazel reacts completely differently; she is happy that her mother will become a "Patrick" (the leader of her support group) as well. They start watching TV and Hazel makes her parents swear that they will not get divorced after her death.

Chapter Twenty-five (30/05/15)

The next morning, Hazel calls her friend Kaitlyn and they talk for a while. It comes to Hazel's mind that Gus might have sent the pages to Van Houten. She asks Lidewij right away via email. Lidewij answers and tells her that she is going to look for them right now. While Hazel waits for an answer she gets very sad about her not having a future with Gus. Her mom comes in and tells her that they are celebrating Bastille Day in the park. After they had picnic in the park they visit Gus's grave. When she gets home she checks her emails and finds an email from Lidewij – it has four files attached. When she opens it, she realizes that it is not an ending to *An Imperial Affliction* but a eulogy for her. The end of the eulogy is: *"You don't get to choose if you get hurt in this world,[...] but you do have some say in who hurts you. I like my choices. I hope she likes hers."* She does.

Hazel Graze Lancaster – From the beginning of the book, Hazel appears very mature. Her thoughts are very conscientiously and deep. In the scene when she meets Kaitlyn, the contrast to a mediocre teenager is very obvious. While Kaitlyn is talking about boys and shopping, Hazel Graze thinks about stuff that really matters in her life. One of Hazel's big fears is to hurt anyone. Being a vegetarian symbolizes that. She often thinks about what will happen to her parents and Augustus if she dies. She desperately wants to find out what happens to the characters of *An Imperial Affliction* after the end, because she wants to make sure that Anna's parents in the book can life a happy life. If they can then her parents could as well. Her physical condition gets worse during the book. At the beginning she talks about not taking the elevator to support group because that is what people do who are about to die. In the end she is the one who can't take the stairs anymore. In the beginning of the book, Hazel does not really want to dare a relationship with Augustus, but in the end she is happy that she did, as we see in the very last sentence of the book.

Augustus "Gus" Waters – see on profile

Isaac – Isaac is a friend of both main characters, Hazel and Gus. He is naturally sarcastic and cynic. He makes a lot of jokes about himself being blind. He is incredibly devastated when his girlfriend, Monica, dumps him.

Mrs. Lancaster – Hazel's mother is the parent who spends most of her time with Hazel. Hazel is always afraid that her mom won't have a life after her death so she is really happy when she finds out that her mom is taking classes to become a social worker.

Mr. Lancaster – Hazel's dad is a very emotional person, he breaks out into tears several times in the book. He is the one who earns the money in the Lancaster family. He is at work a lot.

Peter Van Houten – Peter Van Houten is a crucial character. He wrote the book *An Imperial Affliction* and he lost his daughter Anna at the age of 8 from Leukaemia. He is an alcoholic and he insults everyone and everything that has to deal with him. But even though he appears as an incredibly bad person during the whole book, he shows some heart when he comes to Gus's funeral. He still behaves like an "asshole" there but at least he shows up. Apart from that he is kind of a genius which you can recognize at the way he speaks and writes.

Patrick – Patrick is the leader of the support group. He is always optimistic and he strongly believes in god and an afterlife.

Augustus's parents – We don't really get to know a lot about them. They are very friendly people and they love Hazel.

Lidewij Vliegenthart – She is Van Houten's assistant. She is different to Van Houten and does not like his aggressive and offensive character.

Kaitlyn – She is one of Hazel's friends and a former schoolmate. They are still friends but because of the cancer, they live in different worlds.

Monica – Monica is Isaac's girlfriend. Later she becomes his ex-girlfriend because she can't handle him being blind.

"I'M ON A ROLLER COASTER THAT ONLY GOS UP" – AUGUSTUS WATERS
Augustus Waters

General facts:
Age: 17
Hometown: Indianapolis, USA
Cause of death: Osteosarcoma

Outward appearance:
Hair colour: Mahogany hair
Eye colour: Blue
Physique: Leanly muscular
Specialities: Right leg has been replaced by a prosthesis

Characteristics:
Fears: Oblivion; dying without leaving a mark
Loves: Metaphors; Storm-trooper-zombie-books; An Imperial Affliction; Hazel Graze
Hates: Basketball (Everyone thinks he likes it)

In the book, you can find two different versions of Augusts Waters. In the beginning it is the incredibly self-confident, strong, funny and charming boy. His goal in life is to set a mark for the world he's leaving. He loves talking and when he is in the "Funky Bones Park" with Hazel for the first time, we can see how much he over-plans the things he does. He is very into metaphors, like the cigarette thing and when he jumps on a grenade in a video game to save children. When his cancer returns, his façade falls apart. He is very afraid now of being not able to do something extraordinary and he doesn't like that he is not able to play his role anymore. Augustus turns into Gus and Hazel learns to love the new Gus even more than Augustus. His metaphor, the cigarette, stays his symbol through the whole book. It resembles the control he would love to have over everything that could kill him. With the cigarette in his mouth he feels stronger. For instance, he puts one in his mouth when he is on a plane for the first time. As we get to know in the eulogy he wrote for Hazel, he accepts his decisions and he is not worried about not being extraordinary anymore.

For me, the most moving scene was when Hazel and Augustus kissed in the Anne Frank House. After the scene with Peter Van Houten, which made me somehow really angry, it was like the atmosphere in the book was completely dark and sad. I could really identify with Hazel when she got into the Anne Frank House and tried to climb all the stairs on her own. I could feel the anger and hatred she had because of what Van Houten did to them. She wanted to prove to herself that she can still do it and also she thought that she owed it to Anne Frank. Hazel thought that if Anne Frank was able to be quiet and not complain about her situation, she cannot complain about hers. Hazel wanted to do it as well to show her respect. When they eventually arrived at the top, the situation reached its peak and I felt like something had to happen. I actually didn't expect the kiss (I couldn't remember it from the movie) and that's probably why I liked this scene so much. I actually expected that Hazel would faint but the kiss was the complete opposite and it turned the exciting situation n a very beautiful one. Of course I always waited the whole time for them to finally start a real relationship.

Sunday, 12th of May 2012

Sh*t. I haven't felt so bad since the doctor told me that I'm gonna be blind. Today, Augustus asked me whether I could write him a eulogy. I mean it's actually clear that he is not going to live much longer but, dammit, I just don't want him to fuc**ng pass away. I knew that this day would come but I just blocked it out. I didn't want to think about his death, I mean we've been friends since we've still worn nappies and now all this is just going to end?? I can't believe that sh*t. It's like a part of me is dying. I want to scream, I want to shout I am sooo angry!!!! I'm angry about the world, I'm angry about everything! It just sucks!!! I would do anything to change with him. I can't stand the thought of a world without him and I don't want to see Hazel suffering not just from cancer but from him being dead! I really like her and I know how much she loves him, like she probably loves him more than I used love Monica (that bitch, I hate her). If Augustus dies, she will probably die with him. But obviously I don't deserve it. It's like Augustus always tells me: Life is no wish-granting factory, it's a very mean and nasty place and it doesn't care how tough you are it will beat you to your knees and keep you there permanently if you let it. I have to fight it. My life has to go on. And I'd give everything to give Augustus my life. I'm still afraid of starting to write the eulogy because I feel like that's the last step to finally say goodbye and give up the hope. I fuc**ng love this arrogant bastard so much! He means more than a brother to me.....   Well that's probably the most messed up entry I've ever written but I just can't control myself at the moment it's so crazy.

I just want everybody to be happy again. Why can't we just be happy? Why? Why? I can't see why! Dammit I can't stop crying. I have to stop that I just can't think about it anymore... If there just was anything I could do about this situation. I should really start to write this freaking eulogy now....

Don't leave me Augustus. Don't leave me. For me you are the heroic, remarkable, extraordinary bastard you always wanted to be. Just don't leave me yet. Don't leave. Don't

....Isaac

The ending – I really can't imagine a better ending for the book. There are only two other possibilities how the book could end and I will explain why the one chosen by John Green is the best. First, Hazel could die. This is the possibility which is probably the one most people expect. From the beginning until Augustus's cancer returns, Hazel Graze is the sickest person in the book. There are a couple of scenes where her condition is really critical. If she died instead of Gus, the book would be less exciting and it would not make us so crazy about it. It would just be an average book without any significant specialities. The other possibility is that none of them dies. Some people would probably like this version but I personally hate exaggerated happy endings. The whole book would not make any sense if in the end they both survived. It just would not be very close to the reality. Certainly there are cases where people with terminal cancer do survive, but unfortunately this is not the standard situation. Most of them die and that's why I think the book is pretty close to the reality. Another point is that the book would be way less dramatic and simultaneously way less fascinating if both survived. In addition to that I really like the very ending, when Augustus as well as Hazel Graze, admit that they are happy with the choices they have made and that they don't regret anything.

To put it in a nutshell, John Green did a marvellous job by letting Augustus die in the end (even though this sounds mean) and letting Hazel accept the choices she made.

The book – I nearly liked the book as much as I liked the ending. Through the whole book there were never any scenes where I hoped that the chapter finally is over because it's boring. You know the books where you desperately wait for the end of the chapter so that you can finally put the book away because it is only so little interesting? *The Fault in Our Stars* is not one of these books. As I already mentioned, I am not a big fan of fictional literature, but I really liked the book though. One reason is that it is really realistic. Nothing is exaggerated and I think everything from the book could happen more or less the same way in reality. Another thing is, that the love between Gus and Hazel is not represented in this "oh-my-god-I-love-him-so-much-I-could-eat-him"-way. Instead, a bigger range of feelings, superficial as well as deep feelings, are described. Additionally, I love the humour of the book. Gus's exaggerated self-confidence, Isaac's cynical comments and Hazel's brainy phrases make the book very rich in variety and gave me quite a few good laughs. My last point is the terrific ending. As I already mentioned, I can't think of a better way to design the ending.

All in all, I would give the book eight out of ten stars.

SOME INFINITIES ARE BIGGER

THAN OTHER INFINITIES.

OKAY?

THE FAULT

OKAY.

WHAT A SLUT TIME IS. SHE SCREWS EVERYBODY.

THE MARKS HUMANS LEAVE

ARE TOO OFTEN SCARS.

IN OUR STARS

THE WORLD IS NOT A WISH-GRANTING FACTORY.

YOU PUT THE KILLING THING RIGHT BETWEEN YOUR
TEETH, BUT YOU DON'T GIVE IT THE POWER TO DO
ITS KILLING.

MAYBE 'OKAY' WILL BE OUR 'ALWAYS'

BY JOHN GREEN

YOU GAVE ME A FOREVER WITHIN THE NUMBERED
DAYS, AND I'M GRATEFUL.

"BUT IT'S NOT A CANCER BOOK"